the
princess
saves
herself
in
this
one

the
princess
saves
herself
in
this
one

amanda lovelace

Andrews McMeel
PUBLISHING®

for the boy who lived.
thank you for inspiring me to be
the girl who survived.
you may have
a lightning bolt
to show for it,
but my body is a
lightning storm.

⚡

trigger warning

this book
contains
sensitive material
relating to:

child abuse,
intimate partner abuse,
bullying,
sexual assault,
self-harm,
eating disorders,
queerphobia,
menstruation,
alcoholism,
racism,
trauma,
death,
suicide,
grief,
cancer,
fire,

& possibly
more.

remember
to practice self-care
before, during & after
reading.

contents

warning I:

this is not a
fairy tale.

there is no
princess.

there is no
damsel.

there is no
queen.

there is no
tower.

there are no
dragons.

there is simply
a girl

faced with the
difficult task

of learning to
believe in

herself.

warning II:

happy ending
ahead.

here lie
the raw,
unpolished,
& mostly
disjointed
pieces of
my soul.

ah, life—
the thing
that happens
to us
while we're off
somewhere else
blowing on
dandelions
& wishing
ourselves into
the pages of
our favorite
fairy tales.

once upon a time . . .

I. the princess

~~the princess~~ i was born
a little bookmad.

i could be found stroking
the spines of my books

while i sat locked alone
inside my ~~tower~~ bedroom.

all the while, i hoped my books
would spill their exquisite words

over the lush green carpet
so i could collect them one by one

& savor them like
berries inside my mouth.

- *forever a collector of words.*

when i had
no friends
i reached inside
my beloved
books
& sculpted some
out of
12 pt
times new roman.

- & it was almost good enough.

the little girl
isn't listening to you—

she's way too busy
staring out the window,

fantasizing about
a world of

magical accidents,
flying envelopes,

screeching owls,
adoring giants,

brooms that
do more than sweep,

friends who are
always loyal,

& a train
that will take her

to an enchanted place
far far far

away from
here.

- put under a lifelong spell.

~~the queen~~
my mother
smiled
as she offered
a cube of
sugar
in her
upturned palm.

greedily,
i accepted.

i reached inside
my mouth,
delicately placing one
(just one)
on the center
of my tongue,
& i clamped
down.

salt.

that is what abuse is:
knowing you are
going to get salt
but still hoping for sugar
for nineteen years.

- you may be gone, but i still have a stomachache.

one night,
~~the princess~~
~~i~~
~~the princess~~
~~i~~
~~the princess~~
~~i~~

the princess woke
to feel her castle rocking

    back & forth
back & forth
        back & forth

            back & forth
          back & forth
              back & forth

    back & forth
back & forth
        back & forth

at first,
she thought
a hurricane
must be brewing,
but she was
wrong.

where
do all the
memories go,
the ones we
hide away
with
lock &
key yet
continue
to shape
us all the
s a m e?

- *did it really happen if i can't remember it?*

at eleven years old
the doctor weighed me
& afterward,
my mother told me
i was too fat
& that i needed to
go on a diet
immediately.
for an entire year,
food barely passed
through my lips.
i did not even allow myself
to take a sip of water
because i wanted to be
so thin that i
could blow away
with the slightest breeze—
d i s a p p e a r .
i dropped sixty pounds
in a few short months
& i had to wear long sleeves
to cover up my
only catharsis.

- *everybody told me how good i looked, though.*

there are
some mothers
who will warn you

to never ever
(ever ever)
touch the stove,

but there are
some mothers who
will drag you right to it

kicking & screaming,
laughing
as they

watch the flames
lick at your
fingertips.

- when you're taught to see the world through
fire, nothing looks safe.

"friend request from _____"

    a) the girl who said you were ugly.
    b) the girl who said your voice was off-key.
    c) the girl who refused to defend you.
    d) the girl who laughed at you behind your back & to your face.
    e) the girl who took your lunch money every day because she said you didn't need to eat.
    f) the girl who said you were "fat" even after you starved yourself half to death.
    g) the girl who was supposed to be your best friend.
    h) all of the above.

- keep pressing ignore, lovely.

16

fat
\\'fat\\
adjective

    1: a descriptive word.
        it has no deeper meaning.
        it should not determine
        the worth
        (or lack thereof)
        of a human being.

- what i know now that i wish i knew then.

sticks & stones
never broke

my bones,

but words
made me
starve myself
until

you could
see all of them.

- *skin & bone.*

my sister & i
spent our nights
wishing upon
the plastic
glow-in-the-dark
stars
plastered to our
ceiling.

- *we made it after all.*

there
was never
enough alcohol
to keep my mother warm
in a house
as cold as
t   h   i   s.

- *but you kept trying, didn't you?*

you should
never love
                    anything
more than
you love
your own
children.

you should
never love
                    anyone
more than
you love
your own
children.

- how could you?

now that i
think about it,

she always did
make sure

i was watching
while she pried

the balloon
out of my hand

&
let it

f l o a t   a w a y.

there were
once
~~six~~ five
girls
who
shared
every part
of themselves:

blood
&
secrets
&
lovers
&
even
a diary.

but
a girl
can only
bleed
so much
before she
meets
her demise.

- *i'll see you in california.*

how can
someone
be
too young
to be
in love
when we were
crafted
from
                    ocean waves
                    & starlight?

- *young love.*

one morning
i woke up

with my favorite
wizard boy sheets

sticky with
the blood

i begged would
never come,

& suddenly
it was like

my body was
no longer my own

but everyone
else's.

- *not much has changed since then.*

my first kiss:
        tackled,
        pinned down,
        a mouth
        repeating
        no no no.

after:
        bruises
        &
        the unmistakable
        taste of
        blood.

- i will never forgive you.

you have
been the
star
of each
& every
one of
my
nightmares.

- *you left but you stayed.*

i'm sorry
if i
wasn't
the daughter
you had
in mind.

- i only ever wanted to make you proud.

I.
the sight
of red ribbon
spooling
underneath
the stinging bite
of steel.

II.
the
once too-tight
jeans
hanging
off
my body.

- *two unexpected reliefs for a girl.*

it is strange
how

s
i
s
t
e
r
s

can
be

s
a
v
i
o
r
s

or

s
t
r
a
n
g
e
r
s

&
sometimes
a bit of both.

- *sisters.*

there were
some secrets

that threatened
to chip away

at my
porcelain pieces

but felt necessary
to keep myself

whole.

- *i didn't know anything.*

- silence has always been my loudest scream.

the princess counts:

1. the scabs on her knees.
2. the number of sky-high swings.
3. the books on her shelves.
4. the loose threads on her shirt.
5. the letters in her words.
6. the tiles on the ceiling.
7. the seconds that pass her by.
8. the missed homework assignments.
9. the hours till she'll crawl back into bed.
10. the pounds on the scale.
11. the number of times she chews.
12. the light echoes of her steps.
13. the tally marks drawn on her body.
14. the strands of hair that fall out.
15. the stars that dim.

& then she starts over.
& then she starts over.
& then she starts over.
& then she starts over.
& then she starts over.

birds
can't
                    f l y   a w a y
when you
clip
one of
their wings.

you
weren't
satisfied
with just
clipping
one of
my wings.

you tore
both
out from
the root
to make sure
i could
                    n e v e r   f l y
anywhere
ever
again.

- *mother & daughter.*

since
i couldn't
have
my wings,
i wore
the
fake ones
dipped
in
gold
glitter.

- a wannabe faerie in converse.

there came
a time
when
poetry
showed me
how to
bleed
without
the demand
of blood.

- my most loyal lover.

i used to think
i was broken

because
i never once

spent my
daydreams

plucking
swollen pomegranates

from
someone else's tree.

- *then i learned that society is broken, not me.*

watching
the house
that was
my sanctuary
& my hell
go up in
flames
was
bittersweet
but mostly

just
sweet.

- *a confession.*

if a house
does not
automatically
make a home,
then a body
doesn't
automatically
make a home
either.

- *i've always felt like a stranger in my skin.*

she begins
tearing
the pages

from the spines
of her favorite
books

& frantically
stuffs wads of words
into her mouth,

praying it's true
that you become
what you eat

while she sucks
the flavor of ink from
her blackened fingertips.

- can't i just be a paper girl with a paper life?

you may
not have left
(many) bruises
on my skin,
but you left giant
blackberry bruises
all over
my soul.

- *i still wonder who i would have been.*

the princess
locked herself away
in the highest tower,
hoping a knight
in shining armor
would come to her
rescue.

- i didn't realize i could be my own knight.

II. the damsel

the damsel
let the dragons
swoop down
& steal her away
from the ugliness
of her world.
unbeknownst to her,
she was only trading
one tower
for another.

- *the wickedest liars of all.*

i'm not scared
of the monsters

hidden underneath
my bed.

i'm much more scared
of the boys

with messy brown hair,
sleepy eyes,

& mouths
that only know

how to form
half-truths.

- *my dragons.*

remember when
you told me
you wrote that
beautiful song
for me
& only me—
your
"only one"?

well,

i'm willing
to bet
you don't
remember
that you had already
showed it to me,
saying it was
for *her.*

- you were in love with the idea of love, not me.

promises
whispered
in the rain
will be washed
a
w
a
y.

- right down the fucking drain.

i was the one thing
he had to deny—
the beautiful truth
within his
terrible lie.

- *who knew such a young heart could shatter?*

when
my dragon
with the
green eyes
left,

i
took
a knife
& cut off
all my long,
pretty hair,
taking away
the only thing
he
ever
loved
about
me.

- *over before it began.*

"i
could
just
eat
you
up."

- *from the insatiable mouth of the big bad wolf.*

he loves me.
he loves me not.

      he loves her.
      he loves her not.

he loves me.
he loves me not.

      he loves her.
      he loves her not.

he loves me.
he loves me not.

      he loves her.
      he loves her not.

he loves me.
he loves me not.

      he loves her.
      he loves her not.

he loves me.
he loves me not.

- i ran out of petals.

blood
runs
wherever
his
fingertips
graze
me.

- *my steel & thorns.*

for a time,
it seemed to me
that we were
                    starlight-touched,
failing to
realize that
we were actually
                    star-crossed.

- the stars were never on our side.

he was made of fire
& i was made of ice.

i came too close to
his flame

& he melted me
with his embers,

reducing me down
to a puddle.

with time,
i froze over again,

but i was never
quite the same—

a fragile, watery imitation
of what once was.

- *where was my fear of fire when it came to you?*

"i hate you."

- *his version of "i love you."*

when
it finally
came
time for
him to
leave,
he
packed up
all my
poetry
in a
suitcase
& took it
with
him.

- first my heart, then my words.

he
promised
to fix me
&

     he left me

more

    s h a t t e r e d

than i had been
before.

- but now i've got gold in the cracks.

i have to
believe
the day
will come
where i don't
               flinch
whenever
i hear
his name.

- *some names will always be cursed.*

i have
so much love
to give,
but no one
ever wants
it.

- *a cup overfilled.*

if
love
is a
battlefield,
then i
must have
forgotten
all of
my armor
at
home.

- a war i never agreed to fight.

in all
my dreams
i could find
myself
picking
my teeth
out of
the
carpet.

- what does the dream dictionary say?

my
mom
told the
nice doctor
she was seeing
starbursts
in her eyes
& they were
almost
beautiful
to her—
like the
fourth of
july
had decided
to come
early.

the doctor
hesitated
before
breaking the news
to her.

"those aren't
stars.

it's cancer."

- *forty years a smoker.*

it was
while we were
drinking our
usual
late-night
coffee.
without
a tremble
in that
gravelly voice
of hers,
she turned
to me
& said
her last
dying wish
was for me
to spread her ashes
over the ocean
so she could
finally go
back
home.

- *a mermaid escapist.*

when your mother
begins to forget
your name,
you begin
to wonder
if you exist
at all.

- stage 4, terminal.

you will think
your parents are

      s h a t t e r p r o o f

until one day
you find out

      t h e y a r e n ' t.

- *what it really means to lose your innocence.*

i'm sick to death
of everyone
telling me
how strong
i am.

me?
strong?

i only act strong
because it's
the only distraction
i have from the
thoughts of

my inevitable
motherless life.

- *a feather disguised as steel.*

everyone
urges me to
hold on to
my dreams
to pass the
time,

but
what happens
when your dreams
are nightmares
stuck on
repeatrepeatrepeat?

- *please wake me up.*

who
will
i
be
without
her?

how
can
i
be
without
her?

irony:
when your
healthy
& intelligent
& strikingly
beautiful
sister dies
less than
a month
before
your terminally ill
mother.

- *nobody realized you were just as sick.*

minutes
before
your mother
made the
death call,

i
smelled
your
warm vanilla
perfume

& my
mouth
filled with
the taste
of dirt.

- *death is one of the senses.*

children are not
meant to die
before their
parents.

          i was not
          meant to grow
          older than
          my eldest sister.

we were meant
to be
four sisters,
not three.

          you were not meant
          to be a can of ashes
          on your mother's
          bedside table.

after all,
you were the one
who always burned
the brightest.

- *fate is a fucking lie.*

the worst
part is never
being able
to know
if it was a
        s u i c i d e
or not.

- *the truth will free me.*

she
once
made a
promise
to
save
me

when
all
along

we
should have
been
saving
her
from
herself.

- *please come back.*

sister—
wherever
you are now,
i hope there is
a beach.

- *starfish will always remind me of you.*

i hold
the seashell
up to my ear,

not with
the anticipation
of hearing
the crash of
the ocean waves

but with
the crushing hope
of catching even the
smallest note
of your voice

one
last
time.

- *immortalized by a voicemail.*

fuck you,
cancer,

for taking away
the possibility

of the mother
i will never

ever get to
have now.

- 11/03/10.

i was the one
who found your body

(*you* were nowhere
to be found),

mouth opened
wide enough

to suck all the oxygen
from the room,

wide enough
to plant lilies in,

wide enough to have
been calling my name—

that is, if only you
remembered it.

- *i want to forget, forget, forget.*

your
death certificate
makes
the claim
that
you died on
november 3rd
at 3:03 a.m.
that is a
lie.
you died
long
before that.

- 3 isn't my lucky number anymore.

when
a loved one
dies,
they say
you should
open a window
to let out
that final
wheezing
breath
so their soul
can
be
set free,
but hers is
still here
with me.
night
after night
after night,
she pounds
her fists
on the walls
of my dreams,
begging for
me to tell
her
the way
out.

- *the other side.*

one funeral:
        tears of grief
        for a life lost
        too young,
        too soon—
        a tragedy.

the other:
        tears of relief
        for a suffering
        that lasted
        far too long—
        a mercy.

- & yet both hollowed me out.

for the
better half
of a year
i was terrified
every time
the phone rang
in case
it was another
death call.

- *three more would come.*

everyone i love leaves.

how many
funerals can
someone attend
before they turn
nineteen?

- the cursed family.

i never
expected
death
to be my most
faithful companion,
but she is
the only one
who will come
without
having to be
asked.

- *the only one who will never leave.*

grief
clung to
her
like an
old,
itchy,
faded,
ill-fitting,
hand-me-down
dress.

death

wound

                    itself

around

her

                  bones

like

a

                  piece

of

red

                 ribbon.

an image:

a girl
with bruises
underneath
her eyes
from sleeping too much
or too little.

a girl
with a
brokenhearted cat
permanently
cradled in her
arms.

a girl
ignoring the piles
of treasured books
surrounding
all sides
of her.

a girl
unable to bring
herself to cry
because if she
finally cries
then that means

it really happened.

is
there
such a
thing
as
dead
mother's day?

months after
my mom
died,
i found the book
she was
reading
last
with a yellowing
receipt
still tucked inside,
marking her place,
& it finally
hit me

you
will never
get to finish
this particular book
you will never
get to start
or finish
another book
ever again
you will never
get to see me
graduate
from college
you will never
meet the love
of my life
you will never
be there for my
wedding
you will never
read these words

we will never
ever ever ever
sit on the back porch
& swap ghost stories
over steaming
coffee mugs
ever
ever
ever
again.

&
i try to
imagine
what you
would
say
if i
told you
i haven't
been able to
laugh
in the
longest time
because whenever
i do
someone tells me
i sound
just like
you,

but
i guess these
are just the
kinds
of things
i'll have to
bottle up
& give to you
later.

- forever a collector of words II.

so many
hours
days
months
years
of my life
were wasted
making sure
i was

h o l l o w

i'm
terrified
down to my
very roots
that there are
parts of myself
that can
never
be

f i l l e d.

*- sometimes i think it would be better if someone
cut the whole tree down & started anew.*

she
won't
stop
haunting
me.

- *my ghost.*

he
won't
stop
hunting
me.

- my ghost II.

fuck the idea
that there is
such a thing
as destiny,
that there exists
some kind of
mysterious master plan,
that there is a god who
simply
does not
give us anything
we cannot
handle.

the pain
did not
make me
a better person.
it did not
teach me not to
take anything
for granted.
it did not
teach me anything
except how
to be afraid
to love anyone.

i am
far too
young
to be so
goddamn
broken
&

if i could go back
in time
& give
myself
her childhood
back,

        i would.

- what was the point?

maybe
i find it
so hard to
believe in

           heaven

because
i don't know
if there

           will be
           poetry

there.

- *legitimate concerns of a mortal.*

i had a
big smile
on my face
as i burned
the bridges
to all the things
i could not
repair.

- does the smoke still choke you?

it took
        losing him
        to finally
        find
        myself.

it took
        losing him
        a second time
        to be sure
        of myself.

that
        was my
        first act
        of
        self-love.

- *i would thank you, but we both know you don't
deserve it.*

who would
i have
been without
the inspiration
behind my

          demons?

- *probably not a poet.*

i am
caught between
mourning
you

&

thinking
your death
saved
me.

- *will you ever be able to forgive me?*

the princess
jumped from
the tower
& she
learned
that she
could fly
all along.

- she never needed those wings.

III. the queen

once upon
a time,
the princess
rose from the ashes
her dragon lovers
made of her
&
crowned
herself
the
motherfucking
queen of
herself.

- *how's that for a happily ever after?*

in my
mind's eye
i always see you
sitting by yourself
at the kitchen table,
smoking your cigarette
& drinking your coffee
& wanting to be
anywhere else
but here
with
us.

- *were you set free?*

maybe
we will meet again
in another place—
a place where
forgiveness grows
as lovely as
the tomatoes you
used to grow
in your
garden.

*- the shiny red hope that gets me through late
nights.*

three generations
of women
sit around the enormous
kitchen table—

some hunched over
cups of coffee,
some hunched over
cups of tea.

despite our many differences,
we are all laughing so hard
that the thunder outside
must compete with us.

she can't sit here
with us anymore
& i'm sure we can all feel
the heaviness of her absence,

but even when every chair is taken
& everyone else has to stand,
it still feels like there will always
be a space for her.

- *your energy cannot be destroyed.*

when
my mother
died
i finally
got to
meet
my father,
who i
had seen
every day
for
nineteen
years.

it's true
what they
say:
the weight
of
shared
grief
can either
bring you
together
or
drive
you apart.

- *it's never too late for a relationship.*

when you choose
to sit upon a
throne
made up of
lies

&
the bodies
of the people who
mistakenly thought
they could

t
r
u
s
t

you,
the only
thing left
to do
is

f
a
l
l.

- *but i bet it was fun while it lasted.*

what ever
will you do
when everyone
stops believing
your
red lipstick-
stained
lies?

- friends can break your heart, too.

oh,
i bet
you regret
making
an enemy
out of
me.

- *one back, two knives.*

you can
hate me
forever
if that's
what you
really want,

but
friends
don't just
let friends
turn into
sleepy dragons,

not
when
the claw marks
were as fresh
as mine
were.

- *hurting others is a choice.*

i wonder
how many times
you touched her
& had to
pretend
it was
me.

- does it still sting?

i hope you
treat her better
than you
ever
treated me.

- you can have my forgiveness, but you can't
have me.

please
believe me
when i say
revenge
was
never
my intention.

- but it still tastes sweeter than honey.

you   the
brought   needle
& i brought the thread.
we meant to mend our
two broken hearts,
but we ended up
stitching them
togeth
er.

if he was
my cup of tea,
then you are
my cup of
coffee.

tea simply
isn't
enough
for me
sometimes,

but
coffee
can get me
through
anything.

- *did i make you up?*

before he left,
he wrapped my heart
in layers of
briars & barbed wire
to make sure
that no one else
could ever get in,
but you were
more than willing
to bloody
your hands
for me.

- *you never even got pricked.*

his talent:
>   he never
>   once
>   had to use
>   his hands
>   to touch
>   each & every
>   part of
>   me.

- he could touch me across highways.

somehow,
my soul
knew
your soul
before we
ever had the
chance
to meet.

- it was like coming home after a long, long day.

i would say
you held the key
to my heart,

but you
never needed
it.

- from the beginning i knew i could leave it un-
locked for you.

I.   he calls me
gorgeous.

II.   he reads
all my
favorite books
& then
asks for
more.

III.   he knows
exactly how
to make my coffee.
("light & sweet,
just like you," i
always joke to him.)

IV.   he asks me
how i am doing
every single day
& he
genuinely
cares to hear
the answer.

V.   best of all,
i know he will
still love me
when he
wakes up
tomorrow morning.

- *five things you made me think weren't possible.*

i say to him,

"we will always
have our octobers.

- *even when everything else fades.*"

he
opened me up
like a book
& poured the
poetry
back into
me.

- my personal pen & paper.

a list of red things:
        I. his hair.
       II. our lips.
      III. my nails.
      IV. our breath.
       V. my sheets.

- worth the wait.

flowers
grow
wherever
his
fingertips
graze
me.

- my sun & rain.

t
h
i
s
:

you & me,
a fading october afternoon,
the biting chill filling up the air,
noses turning rosy at the tips,
drinking our too-sweet coffees,
pinkies hooked together,
forgetting everything
& everyone else.
this, this,
this.

- 10/13/12

my boy?
he is even
better than
books.

- fiction has nothing on you.

meteors
could begin
spontaneously

        p
              o
                    u
                  r
                        i
                              n
                                    g

from
the twilight
sky

& he wouldn't look
even half as
amazed

as he does when
he hears my
laugh.

- *you make me feel like i'm a phenomenon.*

it only takes
a single word
from you

to make me
feel like i
could

command
the world's
armies

&
rule over
queendoms

&
direct
the oceans

&
finally defeat the
winter light.

- *i am strong enough for anything.*

i am so glad
we were born
during the same
lifetime.

- i may not believe in fate, but i believe in you.

i need your
lazy, coffee-drinking
mornings.

i need your
famous french
toast.

i need your
pumpkin-picking
afternoons.

i need your
footsteps following me
as i browse the bookstore (again).

i need your
clothes strewn all over
~~my~~ our floor.

i need your
sidelong looks
only i understand.

i need your
comfortably quiet
midnight moments.

i need
all of
it.

- *you're the real poem, darling.*

his smile makes my bones ache.

- a pain i welcome.

when i see
your light pieces
with
my dark pieces,
i begin to
understand why
they say
opposites attract.

- *chiaroscuro.*

in winter,
it's the snowflakes.

in spring,
it's the raindrops.

in summer,
it's the flower petals.

in autumn,
it's the leaves.

all these things
will eventually fall,

but not one of them
will fall as hard

as i do for you when i
wake up every morning.

- all the clichés were written with us in mind.

i am so sorry
for all the times
the

               darkling
               dragon
               demon

living inside
my darkest
corners
came
roaring out,
flames ready,
hell-bent
on
extinguishing

               all the light
               in you.

- please don't leave.

the constellation
of stars
         s c a t t e r e d
across his
back
is the
map
that guides me
home
each time
i find myself
lost.

- *you are my home.*

I.   a well-loved book.
II.   a cool, overcast day.
III.   a mug of coffee.
IV.   a warm blanket.
V.   you.

- the only things i need to feel free.

he
did not
teach me
how
to love
myself,
but he
was
the bridge
that
helped me
get

      here.

- i thank the universe every day for you.

he walked
me down
the bridge
marked with
our names,
got down
on one
knee,
& opened up
my favorite
book—
the one
with the
beautiful princess
& her own
beloved book
on the cover.

inside,
i found

a tiny,
perfect,
amethyst
hope.

- 't will forever keep.

i
let myself
know
that my life
doesn't
have to be over
just because
theirs are
& i went
ahead
& painted
the sun
back into
my sky.

- *i am allowed to live my life.*

"what are you
going to do with your
english degree?"

        "~~i plan to~~
        ~~crack open~~
        ~~the skulls of the~~
        ~~masses~~
        ~~& plant~~
        ~~a colorful~~
        ~~garden~~
        ~~in every~~
        ~~brain."~~

        "~~i am~~
        ~~going to lace~~
        ~~together~~
        ~~a necklace~~
        ~~of words~~
        ~~for everyone~~
        ~~i meet."~~

        "~~for once~~
        ~~in my life~~
        ~~i am going~~
        ~~to make sure~~
        ~~someone finally~~
        ~~hears~~
        ~~me."~~

"i don't know."

- & it's okay not to know.

fiction:
>
> the ocean
> i dive
> headfirst
> into
> when i
> can
> no longer
> breathe
> in
> reality.

- a mermaid escapist II.

over the decades,
her books became
such a part
of her

that
the ink
somehow escaped
her veins

& bloomed
her favorite
words & images
onto her skin.

now
the world
would have
no doubt:

she
was the
pagebound
girl.

- *page to skin.*

when i die,
do not
waste
a minute
mourning me.
i may go,
but i will
leave behind
all my
thousand & one
lives.

- *a bookmad girl never dies.*

all of the oceans
& galaxies
did not
conspire together to
create me
just so i could
reproduce for
you.

- startling fact #1.

i would like to eat
even just one meal
without feeling

ashamed.

- healing is ongoing.

i would like to look
into a mirror
without immediately

        looking away.

- healing is ongoing II.

if i ever
have a
daughter,
the first
thing
i will
teach her
to love
will be
the word
"no"
&
i will
not
let her feel
guilty
for using
it.

- *"no" is short for "fuck off."*

they say
they only want
flowers
to grow from
my mouth,

so i will
look them
dead
in the
eye

as i
shove
soft petals
past
my lips,

chew
with
my jaw
completely
unhinged,

& spit
them
down
at
their feet.

- *i will never be your expectations of me.*

i am
a tigress
who has earned
her softer-than-velvet
stripes.

- an ode to my stretch marks.

i am
a lioness
who is no longer
afraid to let the world
hear her
roar.

- an ode to me.

i
hope
you
can find it
in your
heart
to be
proud
of the
woman
i have become
in spite
of
you.

- still hoping for sugar instead of salt.

&
the dragon
came flying back
to the girl
(as dragons often do)

expecting to find
the damaged damsel
he left behind
so long
ago.

he was
horrified
to find the
mighty queen
standing before him.

after all,
only queens
have the power
to vanquish dragons
like him.

he dared to
seat himself
upon the throne
she built with her own
two hands

&
tell her she
would never
be strong enough
to rule on her own.

the queen
looked right
into the dragon's face
as she laughed
at his silly words

then
unleashed
upon him
the fire dancing
in her palms.

- *sugar, spice, & fire.*

i will
take the
blood-tipped
thorns
they
stuck
in you
&
from
them
i will
teach you
how to
weave
together
the crown
you
deserve.

- you are stronger than i will ever know.

IV. you

raid your library.
read everything
you can get your
hands on
& then
some.

go on,
collect words
& polish them up
until they shine
like starlight
in your
palm.

make words
your finest weapons—
a gold-hilted sword
to cut your
enemies
              d
                 o
                     w
                         n.

- a survival plan of sorts.

if poetry is
a house

overcome
with flames,

then i'm running
back into it

to save each &
every word

so i can
pass them

along to
you.

- *words should save, not burn.*

trees
have words
the wind
cannot carry,
so we must
write
on them
their stories
until there are
none left
for them
to tell.

- *write the story.*

write the story.

push
your hands
into the dirtiest
parts of yourself.

take the
rot & decay
& turn it into
nourishment & life.

water it
& sing to it
& show it
sunlight.

grow a beautiful garden
from your aching
& teach yourself
how to thrive from it.

write your story.

- the sign you've been waiting for.

1. fill in the blank:
   poetry is _____.

        - *anything you want it to be.*

if you
don't want to
end up in
someone else's
poem,

      then maybe
      you should
      start
      treating
      people
      better
      for
      a
      change.

- an unapologetic poet.

when you live
in new york
or new jersey

it is almost
a rite of passage
when someone
jumps in front
of your train.

the first thought
is always,
"i'm going to be
late for work."
it is never,
"what a tragedy
she felt that
there was no
other way out."

but it is.
it is a fucking
tragedy
when
the world
does not stop
for you
even when
you give it
every last
drop of your
blood.

- i never learned your name, but you mattered to
me.

i walk to
where the road
meets the
sidewalk.

a man
comes up to me,
begging me to
let him know

if i see any
family photos
on the muddy,
littered ground.

he doesn't care
that his home
has been reduced to
a pile of rubble,

that he has lost
every last stitch of clothing,
every last book,
every last electronic.

he
just wants
a way to
remember.

- *hurricane sandy.*

there is not
enough
rainwater
in all
the skies
to rinse
the
innocent
blood
from
your hands.

- *their lives will always matter.*

you were
sent down
from the stars

exactly the way
you were supposed
to be—

the way
you would
love,

the way
you would
lust,

& the way
you would find
your wings—

& no one
should have
been given

the power
to take that
                    away
from you.

- *you deserve your pulse.*

a
world
where all

human beings
are taken care of

shouldn't be called

a "revolutionary"
way of life

& yet
it is.

- *burn.*

we are the generation
you gave participant
trophies to.

we are the generation
you made wear helmets,
elbow pads, & kneepads.

we are the generation
you gave censored CDs
& PG movies to.

we are the generation
you spent years overprotecting
then threw to the wolves.

now we are the generation
running on nothing but coffee
& three hours of sleep.

we are the generation
working minimum-wage jobs
with college degrees.

we are the generation
making just enough
money to survive.

we are the generation
you didn't want to see fail
then ensured that we did.

- *millennials.*

emily—
i often
find myself
wondering
if you are still
out there
trying to find
yourself by
candlelight.

is sylvia there
beside you,
guiding
the way with
the old
brag
of her
beating
heart?

does
virginia
have
a room
all her own?
& what about
harriet
& anne
& harper?

does
a woman
ever
find
her peace?

or is death
our only
feather-covered
hope?

- *i'll be there with matches.*

your hips
will try to burst
through your skin.

your thighs
will try to grow together
like a mermaid's tail.

a soft garden
will try to sprout
on your legs.

(& between your legs,
on your upper lip,
on your armpits, etc.)

no, you are
not just here to be
sexy for him.

the world begins
& ends
when you say so.

- *what they don't want you to know.*

food
is
not
the
enemy.

- *society is.*

if you ever
look at
your reflection
& feel the desire
to tell yourself

you're not
good enough,
beautiful enough,
skinny enough,
curvy enough,

then i think
it's about time
you smashed
that mirror
to bits,

don't you?

- *use those fragments to make stepping-stones to
your own self-love.*

i'm
pretty sure
you have

                    s t a r d u s t

running
through
those

                    v e i n s.

- *women are some kind of magic.*

I. you will
    come across people
    who simply cannot wait
    to watch you fail.

II. there will be many times
    in which you
    will fail
    (miserably),

III. but your failures
     are just what happened—
     they don't have to be
     who you are.

IV. all you can do is
    take those mistakes
    & use them as fertilizer
    to help you grow.

V. you have to
    keeping moving forward
    no matter what
    their voices say.

- this life is still worth living.

the leaves
are going to
change.

the leaves
are going to
spiral to the
ground.

the leaves
are going to
return better
than ever
before

& darling,
so are
you.

so are
you.

- *autumn certainties.*

you
are not
obligated
to have
children
just because
your body
has that
capability.

you
are so
so
so
much more
than the
possibility
of
children.

you give
birth
to oceans
        every
        single
        day.

- your friendly neighborhood man-hater &
child-eater.

be a
mermaid.

be a mermaid
who doesn't settle
for making a
small splash.

be a
mermaid
who doesn't
stop until she makes
tidal waves.

be a
mermaid
who knows to
stop before
she devastates
the world with her
tsunamis.

- *don't allow the world to take your kindness.*

you
did
absolutely
nothing
to
deserve
it.

- fuck rape culture.

repeat after me:
you owe
no one
your
forgiveness.

- except maybe yourself.

the love
some girls
have for
other girls
is
so gentle
& so soft
& so fucking
beautiful,
&
these girls
deserve
to have
better stories
than the ones
where they
are murdered
because they love
with too much
of their
hearts.

- *love is never a weakness.*

the only thing
required
to be
a woman
is to
identify
as one.

- *period, end of story.*

your happiness
comes before

anyone else's
happiness.

- the real meaning of "self-respect."

just because
they don't
hit you
doesn't mean it
isn't
abuse.

wouldn't you
think it
a crime
to look up
at
the night sky
& tell
the stars
that they have
no sparkle?

guess what?
you shine
brighter
than all the
starlight
there has
ever been
or ever
will be.

- *emotional abuse is still abuse.*

you're right—

you tried
& you tried
& you tried
& then you tried
some more,

but maybe
they just don't
have it in them
to love you
after all.

now i ask you:
so fucking what?

- *the only love you need is your own.*

you deserve
someone
who makes
you feel
like the
otherworldly
creature
you are.

- *yourself.*

be wary
of the boys who

only ever tell
half-truths

because they
will only ever be

half in love
with you.

- *slay those dragons.*

make
no mistake:

there will
be dragons.

what they don't
know is that

you will always
be ready with

coal wedged
between your lips

& a match poised
between your fingers.

here is the vital difference
between you:

they burn to kill,
but you burn to survive.

- may they never underestimate you again.

when
someone
offers to
save you
make it
your mission
to
        save yourself.

- i believe in you.

the end.

dearest reader,
you have
now
reached
the end of
my story.

i want to
thank you for
going on this
exhausting
journey
with me.

please know that
for every word
you read,
it gets that much
easier for me to
b r e a t h e.

- amanda lovelace

⏳

pending:
your own happy ending.

- *you'll get there.*

special acknowledgments

I. *my sun & rain,* who believed i could write this even when i didn't.

II. *my father,* who probably didn't know i was a writer but will hopefully be proud of me for writing this.

III. *my sister-savior,* who wouldn't imagine giving up on me even in the darkest of times.

IV. *the rest of my family,* who always encouraged me to keep moving forward even if it meant pushing me out of my comfort zone.

V. *my beta readers (christine, mira, danika, shauna, rob, mason, lauren, & michaela),* who cried while reading this &—most important—pointed out my inconsistences & corrected most of my grammar mistakes.

about the author

amanda lovelace is a poetess & storyteller whose words have been shared in her local coffee shop & her tumblr blogs. she currently lives in new jersey with her fiancé. she received her AA in english literature from brookdale community college in 2014 & is working toward her BA in english literature & sociology at kean university. what she will do next, nobody knows—not even her. for now, you can find her reading anything she can get her hands on, writing while she should probably be paying attention in class, thinking about writing but not actually writing, drinking an inordinate amount of coffee, & blogging about books. on top of all this she is a lover of all things cat-related as well as a staunch mermaid enthusiast. she considers herself to be a feminist & a social justice advocate. you can also find her as *ladybookmad* on twitter, instagram, & tumblr.

visit amandalovelace.com

Andrews McMeel Publishing
a division of Andrews McMeel Universal
1130 Walnut Street, Kansas City, Missouri 64106

www.andrewsmcmeel.com

ISBN: 978-1-4494-8641-9

Library of Congress Control Number: 2016955243

Editor: Patty Rice
Designer: Amanda Lovelace
Art Director: Julie Barnes
Production Editor: Erika Kuster
Production Manager: Cliff Koehler

ATTENTION: SCHOOLS AND BUSINESSES
Andrews McMeel books are available at quantity discounts with
bulk purchase for educational, business, or sales promotional use.
For information, please e-mail the Andrews McMeel Publishing
Special Sales Department: specialsales@amuniversal.com.